José María Eguren

THE SONG OF THE FIGURES

Translated by
José Garay Boszeta

José Maria Eguren
Self-portrait, ca. 1910
Canvas streched over cardboard: 320 x 80mm.

CONTENTS

Translator's introduction 9

THE SONG OF THE FIGURES 17

An Interview with José María Eguren
by César Vallejo 105

Index of Poems 111

Translator's introduction

Following the 1911 publication of his first book of poems, *Symbolics*, the very presence of José María Eguren had become a point of contention in the Peruvian literary scene of the early 20th century. With the publication of *Symbolics*, Eguren had single-handedly precipitated a latent tension between traditionalists and innovators in the literary field. There were, on the one hand, the prominent and very well-respected group of established intellectuals, best represented by the conservative critic Clemente Palma, who considered Eguren's poetry to be uninteresting and unworthy of attention; on the other hand, a growing faction of Modernist poets and writers, the likes of José Santos Chocano, Manuel Gonzalez Prada and Abraham Valdelomar ,had immediately recognized a remarkable visionary quality in Eguren's poetry. Unwillingly, to be sure, but perhaps inevitably, Eguren and *Symbolics* had become the subjects of heated debates that often transcended the cultural spheres and reached the volatile substance of a political and generational divide. Almost overnight, Eguren became the watershed of the ongoing struggle between the polarizing forces of tradition and innovation, and there didn't seem to be a possible truce or middle-ground in the polemics. Eguren himself, with his mellow and contemplative character, seems to have prudently stayed at a respectful distance from the chain reactions that his poetry had unintentionally precipitated. But he could certainly feel the tension. As he told a young César Vallejo in an interview a few years later:

— Oh, how much you have to struggle; how much I have been confronted! When I started, friends with some authority on these things, they always discouraged me. And I, as you understand, was finally beggining to believe that I was wrong. Only, some time later, González Prada celebrated my verse.[1]

Ironically, Eguren's persona had itself become a sort of reflection of the themes in his own poetry, a battlefield for the perpetual confrontation between antagonic forces such as darkness and light, infancy and old age, life and death, or more to the point for the analogy, between the conservative past and the transformative future. Be that as it may, as the years went by and the spirits cooled down, nobody was quite sure of what to expect of Eguren's poetry after *Symbolics*. Was Eguren's voice a flower of early spring, destined to wither down and remain as a lovely memory, at best? Or would it grow to become a rich and lively forest?

The appeareance of *The Song of The Figures* in 1916, five years after *Symbolics*, would settle these matters for good and consolidate Eguren's reputation as one of the greatest Latin American poetic

1. *Vallejo, César. La Semana No.2, Trujillo, March 30, 1918.* The present volume includes the complete interview as an appendix.

innovators of the century. If *Symbolics* had presented a carefully constructed poetic voice, *The Song of The Figures* features a fully mature poet in complete command of his style. It represented, without a doubt, a substantial achievement in Eguren's work, and it was unanimously received as a remarkable follow-up to the landmark success of *Symbolics*.

The two books resonate with each other and share a common ground, both thematically and aesthetically, and can certainly be read as complementary parts of a cohesive project. We find here all the staples that characterize Eguren's penmanship: symbolic constructions of tragicomic scenarios, metaphoric transitions of color —blues, greens, reds, purples, yellows—, antitheses of light and darkness and an elegant musical chromatism are well represented in *The Song of The Figures*. We see also a transition towards a preference for Oriental themes, shrouded in mystery and sensuality, in contrast with the medieval fantasies, childhood fables and Nordic mythologies of *Symbolics*. Like a "distant daydream from the East", the Oriental themes proliferate across the book, with mentions of Bengalis, a Ceylon girl, pallid Mongols, Asian belles, Almehs and Avatars. In fact, this movement towards sensuality and mystery is announced from the get-go, in the first verses of the opening poem, and one of Eguren's most celebrated, *The Girl of the Lamplight Blue*:

> *In the nebulous passageway*
> *like magic dream of Istanbul,*
> *her profile gleaming she presents*
> *the girl of the lamplight blue.*

If *Symbolics* had been concerned with showing the inevitable downfall of characters doomed by their innocence, their playfulness and irresponsibility, *The Song of The Figures* is concerned instead with corruption, criminality and sin. A comparison of two of the most representative poems of each book, *John Somersault* and *Jezebel*, respectively, should help us illustrate the difference in tone and themes between the two works. On the one hand, *John Somersault* present us with the tragic fate of a heroic character who, by foolishly pressing his luck, breaks the bond with his fellow mates and finds a horrible death by dismemberment; *Jezebel*, on the other hand, shows us the famed scene of the execution of the stateswoman, a priestly character who has become corrupted and betrayed the social pact warranted by her own royal position. In these two tragic scenarios, Eguren alternates between the two sides of the same story, telling us the tale of human inmoderation that leads to an inevitable death. The theme has changed from the foolish hero to the villain priest, but the hubris, the tragedy and the fateful retribution remain. The mood has also changed from the slightly dark humor of *Symbolics*, which had been characterized by an ambiguous stasis between exhilaration and dissolution, towards a more decidedly gloomier and dismal tone, in which feelings like confusion, defeat and nostalgia come into play amidst the devastating final moments.

In spite of these subtle counterpoints, it would also be productive to focus on the numerous continuities between the two books. To be sure, these two aforementioned modes —the heroic and the tragic— are present across Eguren's work, and we can find numerous instances in both books that suggest us a common concern for expressing multiple variations of the same unitary theme of life and death. Most of the motifs that were already present in *Symbolics* will continue seamlessly in *The Song of theFigures*. The scenes of condemned vessels at sea, for instance, or the recurrence of melancholic, wretched young characters, also populate the poems in this collection. The same can be said of Eguren's creative uses of language, full of internal resonances and stylistic innovations. Eguren turns colors into chromatic adjectives, uses archaisms as ornaments, experiments with anomalous syntactical arrangenmentsm, plays with subtle timbres and liberally borrows from foreign languages (from Italian in particular) to create new words which could serve him to compose the rhythms and musical cadence that characterize his poetry. Eguren is fond of playing with language and creating little aesthetical delights that, in spite of their mellow candidness, constitute gracious challenges for the readers' interpretation. In spite of the severity of his themes, it's definitely a playful and mischievous spirit what guides the pen of the poet. Significantly, a loose poetic troupe that identified themselves with the name of "Los Duendes" (The Goblins), composed mostly of young artists and poets (among them Isajara, Alida Elguera, Emilio Adolfo Westphalen, Martín Adán, Carlos Raygada and Gilberto Owen) would gradually begin to congregate at Eguren's house during the following years, inequivocally inspired by the ways of our gentle trickster. In this sense, to illustrate some of this spirit, we shall quote a verse from the same poem we mentioned above, *The Girl of the Lamplight Blue*:

> *Of incantation in a splurge,*
> *rives elated, vaporous tulle;*
> *and across the night she guides me*
> *the girl of the lamplight blue.*

The second line of this stanza is one of the best examples of Eguren's signature wordcraft. *Hiende leda, vaporoso tul,* is certainly a most uncanny construction in the Spanish original, almost undecipherable at first glance, but that in further analysis, gradually reveals its subtle delicacy with economy and precision. Here Eguren plays with an obscure verb and adjective in order to advance a description of the title character, while keeping a strict metric in the verses and fostering subtle internal phonetic resonances. We hope that our present translation, which has meticulously attempted to preserve the inflections and wordplay of the original Spanish language throught all the poems, will be able to organically transmit some of the remarkable mechanics of the text for our English readers. For Eguren was really a sort of noble language goblin, always searching for the astonishing and unexpected turn of phrase in order to express the authentically uncanny. In this sense, the autobiographical poem *Peregrín Hunter of Figures*, unique in Eguren's work, deserves a special mention. Peregrín was the nickname that Eguren's friends had playfully gave him, due to his habit of setting into endless strolls, real peregrinations across the city for hours on end, from the sunset to the late evening, armed with his mini photographic camera and his notebook, seeking to capture the dwindling light impressions and musical word particles that could become the characters and motifs of his poems. José María Eguren —Peregrín, the goblin—, a true poetic marksman. In honest confession, Eguren has captured for us his own figure with good humor and sincerity.

José María Eguren's remarkable voice constitutes one of those infrequent cases in poetry where, just like Athena sprung out of Zeus' skull, a poet has already a fully formed mastery and vision since his first inception into the world. The publication of

The Song of the Figures in 1916 marked the critical point in which all of these qualities became unquestionably self-evident and highly influential for an up-and-coming generation of young poets and writers, such as José Carlos Mariátegui, César Vallejo and Martín Adán. The present volume has attempted to remain faithful to Eguren's linguistic innovations and aspired to render his unique style into a veritable English translation. We are, of course, completely responsible for the results. The present volume also includes, as an appendix, a translation of a 1918 interview with Eguren, conducted by a young César Vallejo, who had just finished writing his first book of poems, *The Black Heralds*, which would be published the following year. Even though we wish there would have been a photographic registry of this interview, we certainly cannot complain about the mental image of this encounter, which must certainly be one of the most delightful moments of Latin American poetry in the 20th century: The day Vallejo visited Eguren in his little house in Barranco, at "the Virgilian hour, turquoise and energetic green", as the afternoon flew by, carrying along the flashes of music and poetry into the rich silver sea.

José Garay Boszeta

THE SONG OF THE FIGURES
FIGURES
— 1916 —

Al ilustre maestro
Don Manuel González Prada

To the illustrious teacher
Esq. Manuel González Prada

LA NIÑA DE LA LÁMPARA AZUL

En el pasadizo nebuloso
cual mágico sueño de Estambul,
su perfil presenta destelloso
la niña de la lámpara azul.

Ágil y risueña se insinúa,
y su llama seductora brilla,
tiembla en su cabello la garúa
de la playa de la maravilla.

Con voz infantil y melodiosa
en fresco aroma de abedul,
habla de una vida milagrosa
la niña de la lámpara azul.

Con cálidos ojos de dulzura
y besos de amor matutino,
me ofrece la bella criatura
un mágico y celeste camino.

De encantación en un derroche,
hiende leda, vaporoso tul;
y me guía a través de la noche
la niña de la lámpara azul.

THE GIRL OF THE LAMPLIGHT BLUE

In the nebulous passageway
like a magic dream of Istanbul,
her profile gleaming she presents
the girl of the lamplight blue.

She insinuates smiling and agile,
and shines her seductive flame,
from the marvelous seaside
trembles the drizzle on her hair.

With voice childish and melodious
in fresh aroma of birch shrub,
talks of a life miraculous
the girl of the lamplight blue.

With warm eyes of sweetness
and kisses of matutine love,
the beautiful creature offers me
a magic and celestial road.

Of incantation in a splurge,
rives elated, vaporous tulle;
and across the night she guides me
the girl of the lamplight blue.

LOS ÁNGELES TRANQUILOS

Pasó el vendaval; ahora,
con perlas y berilos,
cantan la soledad aurora
los ángeles tranquilos.

Modulan canciones santas
en dulces bandolines;
viendo caídas las hojosas plantas
de campos y jardines.

Mientras sol en la neblina
vibra sus oropeles,
besan la muerte blanquecina
en los Saharas crueles.

Se alejan de madrugada,
con perlas y berilos,
y con la luz del cielo en la mirada
los ángeles tranquilos.

THE TRANQUIL ANGELS

The gale has passed; presently,
with pearls and beryls,
the dawn solitude they sing
the tranquil angels.

They modulate holy songs
in sweet bandolines;
looking at the fallen leafy plants
of gardens and fields.

Meanwhile the sun in the haze
vibrates its tinsels,
in the cruel Saharas
they kiss the whitish death.

They leave in the dawning day,
with pearls and beryls,
and the heaven's light in their gaze
the tranquil angels.

LA SANGRE

El mustio peregrino
vio en el monte una huella de sangre;
la sigue pensativo
en los recuerdos claros de su tarde.

El triste, paso a paso,
la ve en la ciudad dormida, blanca,
junto a los cadalsos,
y al morir de ciegas atalayas.

El curvo peregrino
transita por bosques adorantes
y los reinos malditos;
y siempre mira las rojas señales.

Abrumado le mueven
tempestades y Lunas pontinas,
mas, allí, transparentes
y dolorosas las huellas titilan.

Y salva estremecido
la región de las nieves sagradas;
no vislumbra al herido,
sólo las huellas que nunca se acaban.

THE BLOOD

The withered pilgrim
a trace of blood he saw on the hill;
he follows it pensive
in his afternoon's memories clear.

Step by step, the sad one,
sees it in the sleeping city, white,
at the side of the scaffold,
and as the blind watchtowers die.

The incurvated pilgrim
by worshipping forests he transits
and by the accursed kingdoms;
and sees the red signals always.

Overwhelmed he is moved by
the pontine Moons and the tempests,
but, the traces titillate,
therein, transparent and painful.

And shuddering he dodges
the region of the snows sacred;
he doesn't surmise the wounded
only the traces which are endless.

LAS CANDELAS

Las rubias de las candelas
principian sus tarantelas,
lucen rizado cabello
con argentino destello,
y carmesíes
sus senos tienen rubíes,
y titilantes
son sus pupilas diamantes.

Danzan las blondas beldades
siguiendo sus voluptades,
muestran su locura extraña
alegres como el champaña,
y con ardor,
dichosas mueren de amor.

THE CANDLES

The blondies in the candles
begin with their tarantelles,
they flaunt the curls in their hair
with an argentine glimmer,
and crimson silk
their bosoms have rubies,
and flickering
are their diamond pupils.

The blond beauties are dancing
their voluptuousness following,
they display their madness strange
cheerful like the champagne,
and with ardor,
elated they die of love.

EL CABALLO

Viene por las calles,
a la luna parva,
un caballo muerto
en antigua batalla.

Sus cascos sombríos...
trepida, resbala;
da un hosco relincho,
con sus voces lejanas.

En la plúmbea esquina
de la barricada,
con ojos vacíos
y con horror, se para.

Más tarde se escuchan
sus lentas pisadas,
por vías desiertas
y por ruinosas plazas.

THE HORSE

It comes down the streets,
to the paltry moon,
a horse that was killed
in an ancient feud.

Its shadowy hooves...
it quivers, it slips;
gives a sullen neigh,
with its voices afar.

In the leaden corner
of the barricade,
with the eyes empty
and with horror, it stands.

Much later are heard
its slugglish footsteps,
by deserted ways
and by ruinous squares.

NOCTURNO

De Occidente la luz matizada
se borra, se borra;
y en el fondo del valle se inclina
la pálida sombra.

Los insectos que pasan la bruma
se mecen y flotan,
y en su largo mareo golpean
las húmedas hojas.

Por el tronco ya sube, ya sube
la nítida tropa
de las larvas que, en ramas desnudas,
se acuestan medrosas.

En las ramas de fusca alameda
que ciñen las rocas,
bengalíes se mecen dormidos,
soñando sus trovas.

Ya descansan los rubios silvanos
que en punas y costas,
con sus besos las blancas mejillas
abrasan y doran.

NOCTURNAL

From the Occident the tinged light
it fades, it fades;
and in the valley's bottom it sways
the shadow pale.

The insects that pass across the brume
do float and swing,
and in their long dizziness they knock
the humid leaves.

Up across the trunk it goes, it goes
the clear-cut troop
of the larvae that, in branches nude,
lay down fearful.

On the branches of dimmed promenade
that girdle the rocks,
Bengalis are swinging asleep,
dreaming of their songs.

Now are resting the blond Sylvans
who on mountains and coasts,
with their kisses they smother and gild
the whitened cheeks.

En el lecho mullido la inquieta
fanciulla reposa,
y muy grave su dulce, risueño
semblante se torna.

Que así viene la noche trayendo
sus causas ignotas;
así envuelve con mística niebla
las ánimas todas.

Y las cosas, los hombres domina
la parda señora,
de brumosos cabellos flotantes
y negra corona.

On the feathery bed the restless
fanciulla reposes,
and very grave her sweet, smiling
countenance becomes.

For thuswise comes the night bringing
its unbeknownst causes;
thus it enshrouds with a mystic fog
all the wandering souls.

And the things, the men she dominates
the dreary lady,
of the brumous floating head of hair
and black coronet.

LA MUERTE DEL ÁRBOL

La muerte del sauce viejo
miraban los elefantes,
cerca los montes gigantes.

Al vespertino reflejo,
escuchan, alucinantes,
la muerte del sauce viejo.

Levantan, con pena honda,
la fusca pálida fronda
de galanuras perdidas.

Como los ancianos druidas,
lo cercan ensimismados;
y, en fetiquista concierto,
ululan al sauce muerto,
gigantes, arrodillados.

THE DEATH OF THE TREE

The elephants were watching
the death of the old willow,
close to the giant hillocks.

In the reflection of dawning,
the death of the old willow,
they listen to, in awing.

They raise, with a sorrow deep,
the foliage pallid and dimmed
of forsaken gallantries.

Like the elderly druids,
lost in thought they surround it;
and, in fetishist concert,
they hoot at the willow dead,
as they kneel down, gigantic.

MARGINAL

En la orilla contemplo
suaves, ligeras,
con sus penachos finos,
las cañaveras.

Las totoras caídas,
de ocre pintadas,
el verde musgo adornan,
iluminadas.

Campanillas presentan
su dulce poma
que licores destila,
de fino aroma.

En parejas discurren
verdes alciones,
que descienden y buscan
los camarones.

Allí, gratos se aduermen
los guarangales,
y por la sombra juegan
los recentales.

MARGINAL

On the shore I contemplate
smooth, featherweight,
the stems of water reeds,
with their fine headdress.

The fallen totoras,
with ochre painted,
the green moss they adorn,
illuminated.

The bellflowers present
their pomes which are sweet
that, of fine aroma,
liqueurs they distill.

In couples they discourse
the halcyons green,
that searching for shellfish
they descend and seek.

There, gratefully drowsing off
the huarango trees,
and playing 'round the shadow
the yet unweaned sheep.

Ora ves largas alas,
cabezas brunas
de las garzas que vienen
de las lagunas.

Y las almas campestres,
con grande anhelo,
en la espuma rosada
miran su cielo.

Mientras oyen que cunde
tras los cañares,
la canción fugitiva
de esos lugares.

Now you see the long wings,
and the brunet heads
of the herons that come
from the landlocked lakes.

And the countryside souls,
with a great longing,
they look at their heaven
on the pink foaming.

As they hear it spreading
behind beds of reed,
from those whereabouts
the song fugitive.

EL DIOS CANSADO

Plomizo, carminado
y con la barba verde,
el ritmo pierde
el dios cansado.

Y va con tristes ojos,
por los desiertos rojos,
de los beduinos
y peregrinos.

Sigue por las obscuras
y ciegas capitales
de negros males
y desventuras.

Reinante el día estuoso,
camina sin reposo
tras los inventos
y pensamientos.

Continúa, ignorado
por la región atea;
y nada crea
el dios cansado.

THE TIRED DEITY

Grayish, carminated
and with the beard in green,
loses the rhythm
the tired deity.

And with sad eyes he goes,
the red deserts across,
of the Bedouins
and the peregrines.

He goes through the obscure
blind capital cities
of the black evils
and the misfortunes.

Reigning the blazing day,
he walks without delay
after inventions
and ideations.

Ignored, he carries on
through the atheist region;
and nothing creates
the tired deity.

LA ORACIÓN DEL MONTE

Hoy el doliente esquilón
llama a la santa oración,
en lo más hondo del monte.

Reza el olmo secular,
el afligido sinsonte
y el insecto militar.

Posados en peñas moras,
el milano y el azor
siguen con rudo clamor.

Luego esdrújulo martín
junto a las aguas cantoras,
donde templó su violín.

Con el bordón penitente,
allí, el pálido mongol
reza bañado de sol.

Arcano sueña pedir,
el hombre-planta fakir
rendida la mustia frente.

THE PRAYER OF THE HILL

Today the grieving bell toll
to the holy prayer calls,
into the depths of the hill.

Prays the elm seculary,
the afflicted mockingbird
and the insect military.

Perched on mulberry ridges,
the red kite and the goshawk
follow with a rude clamor.

Then paroxytone fisherking
next to the songful waters,
where he tuned his violin.

Therein, the Mongol pallid
with the penitent bourdon,
prays as he bathes in the sun.

Arcane he dreams of pleading,
submitting the forehead withered
the human-plant like fakir.

De la montaña el varón
dice su bronca oración
desde el ocaso al oriente.

From the mountains the male heir
utters his rugged prayer
from the sundown to the east point.

ELEGÍA DEL MAR

Del alba en la marea, por la costa bravía,
oí unas voces hondas de melancolía,
que negras en las dunas lentamente zumbaban
o por los callejones de las rocas roncaban.
En la playa azulina se difunden cantoras,
en un orfeón de sueños, quejas desgarradoras
y dicen tempestades, dicen tribulaciones,
como los costaneros gritos de los aviones,
y las roncas endechas de cárabos marinos,
y barcarola obscura de los remeros pinos;
que recuerdan los lloros de quillas naufragadas,
o parece que anuncian mis horas desdichadas.
¿Será que determinan, cuando punta la Aurora,
la ruta indiferente de mi barca incolora?
¿De funeral son voces, acaso ya me espera
la onda limpia y helada donde morir quisiera?...

ELEGY OF THE SEA

From the dawn on the tide, through the coast in wilding,
I heard voices of deep-seated melancholy,
that blackened over the dunes slowly they buzzed
or through the alleyways of the rocks they growled.
On the bluish beach they diffuse in singing,
in a glee club of dreams, complaints heartbreaking
and they speak of tribulations, of tempests,
like the coastlining screaming of the airplanes,
and the hoarse dirges of the marine barges,
and obscure barcarole of the rowing ships;
that reminisce the cries of castaway keels,
or they announce my wretched hours, it seems.
Could it be they determine, when the daybreak peaks,
the indifferent route of my colorless ship?
There's funeral voices, perhaps for me awaits
the clean and cold wave where I would die if I may?...

ALMA TRISTEZA

¡Alma tristeza, noche!;
del boudoir las hojas la plegaria
han cantado del amor marchito,
gime su desnudez un aria
en el azul precito,
los mochuelos con indiferencia
cruzan el camarín,
y termina su fosforescencia
en el negro jardín.

¡Alma tristeza, noche!;
sus hijas escucho lamentables
que de angustia cercan el vallado,
la mansión obscura, ¡inolvidables!
¡No volverá el día argentado,
ni la belleza que mi alma adora!;
¡ojos de pesar llenos de aurora!

SOUL SADNESS

Soul sadness, night!;
from the boudoir the leaves have sung
the pleading of withered love,
its nudity an aria moans
in the blue foreseeing,
the owlets with indifference
go across the alcove,
and ends their phosphorescence
in the black garden.

Soul sadness, night!;
its daughters I hear pitiful
that in anguish enclose the rampart,
the dark mansion, unforgettable!
The silvered day will not come back!
neither the beauty which my soul adores!;
Eyes of remorse full of auroras!

FLOR DE AMOR

La bella de Asia
cuida en las noches
su adormidera roja y lacia.

Dulce le ríe,
dulce la espía
la hermosa de melancolía.

Al beso blando,
la flor extraña
fue lentamente despertando.

Y con ardores,
ágil se crispa
como un cobra, llena de amores.

Luego desciende,
y en los labios de la mimosa
deja su sangre venenosa.

FLOWER OF LOVE

The Asian belle
guards in the nights
her poppy blossom wilted and red.

Sweetly she laughs,
sweetly she peeks
the beautiful in melancholy.

The flower strange
to the soft kiss
has slowly started to awake.

And with ardors,
it cringes agile
like a cobra, brimming with loves.

Then it descends,
and in the sweetheart's lips
a poisonous blood it leaves.

LAS NAVES DE LA NOCHE

Naves de la noche
a la costa inglesa
hoy prometen la canción y el recuerdo
de la cingalesa.
Con el divino loto adormecida
en las obscuras brisas de Bengala,
la bella mujer celeste y perdida
que aromaciones de especias inhala.
Naves de la noche,
hoy la sombra llevan de antiguos mares,
con luminosos puntos malabares.

¡Canta cingalesa
las añoranzas del morir dichoso!...
las quillas en su valse melodioso,
hacia la ribera de Albión sombría
su partir resuelven
con melancolía...
¡Las naves de la noche nunca vuelven!

THE VESSELS OF THE NIGHT

Vessels of the night
they promise today
to the English coast memory and song
of the Ceylon girl.
Slumberous with the divine lotus
in the obscure breezes of Bengal,
the beautiful woman celestial and lost
who inhales aromations of spice.
Vessels of the night,
now the shadow from ancient seas they bear,
with the luminous points of Malabar.

Do sing Ceylon girl
the longings of the joyful dying!...
the keels in their melodious dancing,
to the shores of Albion shadowy
resolve their departure
with melancholy...
The vessels of the night never return!

JEZABEL

¡Javé!... llora el pueblo las tribulaciones
con el acento del humano rencor;
llora la raza sus prevaricaciones
bajo una tempestad de obscuro pavor.
En la Santa Sión de las profecías
llora el ungido pueblo de Israel,
en la penumbra y las blondas orgías
donde tiembla y ríe infantil Jezabel.
Por líricos jardines tenues y galantes
gime Palestina músicas orantes,
y el profeta ulula su maldición;
la niña princesa a su amor favorito
de la arrogancia, cede su corazón;
y en los amables dulcísimos alegros,
y en los fervientes preludios del amor,
mira, a su lado, mira, dos canes negros
con sus armaduras llenas de furor.
Es la raza impía que al becerro de oro
da fiesta danzante, da rico tesoro
y sacrifica a los dioses de Baal;
ya las vírgenes hebreas se adelantan
con el sándalo aromoso en sus cabellos,
tienen perlas azulinas en sus cuellos,

JEZEBEL

Yahveh!... The people wail the tribulations
with the accent of human rancor;
the race is crying their prevarications
under a tempest of obscure horror.
In the Saint Zion of the prophesies
cries the anointed people of Israel,
in the half-light and the blondish orgies
where trembles and laughs childish Jezebel.
By lyric gardens gallant and fuzzy
moans Palestine a pleading music,
and the prophet hoots his malediction;
to her favorite love the princess girl
of arrogance, gives her heart away;
and in the gentle sweetest allegros,
and in the fervent preludes of love,
she sees, at her side, she sees, two black dogs
wearing their armors filled with furor.
It is the impious race that to the golden calf
gives a rich treasure, gives a feast in dance
and sacrifices to the gods of Baal;
now the Hebrew virgins are moving ahead
with the aromatic sandalwood in their hair,
they are carrying blueish pearls on their necks,

y rosas de Jericó las abrillantan.
Cálida nube sobre la tierra roja
hierve la sangre en juvenil ardor,...
Jezebel, la divina, al ídolo arroja
rubios joyeles de su albo ceñidor.
¡Oh, Acab! ¡oh, tu nativa pasión hebrea,
tu corte de indolente voluntad!
la danza semidesnuda centellea
con níveo cuerpo brillante de impiedad;
mas, un terror hondo y triste se avecina
a tu reina sagrada; tu Jezabel,
la primera del mundo, joya perlina,
fulgente de Tiro, la ciudad infiel;
en goce de la ilusión y de la audacia
la mujer triunfante, ferviente del Asia,
que abominara de la virtud los hierros;
otra vez contempla los obscuros perros.
Era el sol poniente de la tiranía...
¡oh, Jezabel!; la dura reina impía
en la gloria de su innoble arrogancia,
oye trágico rumor cerca su estancia,
y las sonoras voces de los arqueros;
ya en el pórtico fulminan los aceros;
¡ay, los pálidos semblantes justicieros!
Igneo Acab, sobre su carro abrillantado
ha caído por la flecha atravesado.
Jezabel, cerúlea reina luminosa,

and roses from Jericho embrighten them.
A balmy cloud above the red dust
boils the blood in an ardor of youth,...
Jezebel, the divine, to the idol throws
blond trinkets from her white cincture.
Oh, Ahab! Oh, your Hebrew passion native,
your court of insensitive voluptuousness!
the dance is scintillating half naked
with snow-white body glowing with ungodliness;
yet, a deep and sorry terror draws close
to your sacred queen; your Jezebel,
a pearly jewel, the first in the world,
fulgent of Tyre, city of infidels;
in enjoyment of illusion and the audacious
the triumphant woman, fervent of Asia,
who the irons of virtue abhorred;
once again contemplates the obscure dogs.
It was the setting sun of the tiranny...
Oh, Jezebel!; the harsh impious queen
in the glory of her ignoble disdain,
hears a tragic rumor close to her den,
and the sonorous voices of the archers;
now in the portico strike down the irons;
Alas, the countenances pale and righteous!
Igneous Ahab, atop his chariot embrightened
has fallen now by the arrow punctured.
Jezebel, queen, cerulean and luminous,

el final percibe de triunfos y alegros,
y al morir, con la pupila temblorosa,
¡ay!, mira los canes paladines negros.
¡Javé!... llora el pueblo las tribulaciones
con el acento del humano rencor;
llora la raza sus prevaricaciones
en una tempestad de obscuro pavor.

perceives the end of triumphs and allegros,
and she stares at the black paladin dogs,
alas!, as she dies, with the pupil tremulous.
Yahveh!... The people wail the tribulations
with the accent of human rancor;
the race is crying their prevarications
under a tempest of obscure horror.

LOS DELFINES

Es la noche de la triste remembranza;
en amplio salón cuadrado,
de amarillo luminado,
a la hora de maitines
principia la angustiosa contradanza
de los difuntos delfines.
Tienen ricos medallones
terciopelos y listones;
por nobleza, por tersura
son cual de Van Dyck pintura;
mas, conservan un esbozo,
una llama de tristura
como el primo, como el último sollozo.
Es profunda la agonía
de su eterna simetría;
ora avanzan en las fugas y compases
como péndulos tenaces
de la última alegría.
Un saber innominado,
abatidor de la infancia,
sufrir los hace, sufrir por el pecado
de la nativa elegancia.
Y por misteriosos fines,

THE DOLPHINS

It's the night of the sad remembrance;
in an ample square room,
in a yellow illumed,
at the hour of matins
begins the anguishing counterdance
of the deceased dolphins.
They have rich medallions
velvet furs and ribbons;
in nobility, in smoothness
they are like a Van Dyck canvas;
yet, they do preserve a glimpse,
a flame of woefulness
like the first, like the last whimper.
Profound is the agony
of their eternal symmetry;
now they advance in the beats and the fugues
like tenacious pendulums
of the last felicity.
The vanquisher of infancy,
it is an unnamed Knowledge,
that makes them suffer, suffer for the sin
of the native elegance.
And to mysterious ends,

dentro el salón de la desdicha nocturna,
se enajenan los delfines
en su danza taciturna.

inside the hall of nocturnal misfortune,
the dolphins alienate
in their dance taciturn.

LA NAVE ENFERMA

Era la mañana,
por el mar nielado,
un vapor enfermo,
tristemente ha llegado.

Con agudas voces
y desgarradoras,
tembló su sirena
en las quemadas horas.

Unos hombres raros,
su mercadería
conduciendo al muelle
pasaron todo el día.

Y al morir la tarde
se divisan, lejos,
a las tristes sombras
junto a los aparejos.

Nunca más volvieron
los desconocidos,
¡oh, la nave enferma!
¡ay, los seres queridos!

THE DISEASED SHIP

It was the morning,
by the niello sea,
a diseased steamer,
sorrowfully has reached.

With high-pitched voices
heartbreaking also,
its siren trembled
in the burned-out hours.

And their merchandise,
some unusual men
driving to the pier
they have spent the whole day.

And, afar, are sighted
at evening's ending
the sorry shadows
right next to the rigging.

Never they returned
the unknown beings,
Oh, the diseased ship!
Alas, the beloved ones!

NUBES DE ANTAÑO

¡Nubes de antaño!
que vagaban sobre los quintanares
y encendían el estaño
de agujas y tejares.

Y de la plazuela, dulce grama,
donde las niñas antiguas
jugaban en el panorama
de las tardes exiguas.

Y traéis del oriente
ensueños distantes
o la dormida forma clarescente
en las tardes galantes.

¡Nubes de antaño!
que llenáis de dulces amores
y del goce extraño
de las hetairas flores.

Con las nacarinas alas
nos traéis al bosque del engaño.
¡Son noche de la noche vuestras galas
nubes de antaño!

CLOUDS OF YESTERYEAR

Clouds of yesteryear!
that used to wander above the orchards
and that ignited the tin
of needles and brickyards.

And of the town square, the sweet grama,
where the ancient girls used to
play around in the panorama
of the exiguous afternoons.

And from the Orient you bring
the distant daydreams
or the clarescent form slumbering
in the gallant evenings.

Clouds of yesteryear!
that fill us up with sweet lovers
and with the strange glee
of the hetaerae flowers.

To the forest of deceit
thou bring us with the nacreous wings.
Night of the night are thine gaities
clouds of yesteryear!

LAS PUERTAS

Se abrieron las puertas
con ceño de real dominio;
se abrieron las puertas
de aluminio.

Contaron las puertas
los tiempos de ardor medioevales;
contaron las puertas
con sonido de tristes metales.

Crujieron las puertas,
en bélico tinte sonoro;
crujieron las puertas
a los infantes de yelmos de oro.

Rimaron las puertas
ornadas de sable y de gules;
rimaron las puertas
a las niñas de ojos azules.

Se cierran las puertas
con sonido triste y obscuro;
se cierran las puertas
del Futuro.

THE DOORS

Have opened the doors
with a frown of real domain;
have opened the doors
of aluminum made.

Have counted the doors
the times of medieval ardor;
have counted the doors
with a sound of sorrowful ores.

Have creaked the doors,
in a warlike sonorous tone;
have creaked the doors
to the soldiers with helmets of gold.

Have rhymed the doors
ornate with sabers and with gules;
have rhymed the doors
to the girls with the eyes in blue.

Are closing the doors
with a sound sorrowful and obscure;
are closing the doors
of the Future.

ANTIGUA

De la herbosa, brillante hacienda
en la capilla colonial,
se veían los lamparines
cerca de enconchado misal.
Y solitarias hornacinas
de vetusto color añil
cuatro madonas lineales,
óleos de negro marfil.
Y su retablo plateresco,
sus columnas de similor,
estaban mustias, verdinosas
por el tiempo deslustrador.
Y los pesados balaustres
e incrustaciones de carey
eran de años religiosos;
quizá del último virrey.
Era obra de antiguos jesuitas,
techo de roble y alcanfor,
que despedía de murciélago
un anciano y mustio olor.
Sus caprichosos ventanales
veían pesebre y pancal
donde trinaban golondrinas

ANCIENT

From the grassy, shiny hacienda
inside the colonial chapel,
close to a pearl engraved missal
one could see the little lanterns.
And of a hoary indigo
the solitary crevices
four linear madonnas,
black ivory oil paintings.
And its columns of pinchbeck,
its altarpiece plateresque,
were whitered, greenish
by the time lusterless.
And the heavy balusters
and tortoiseshell inlays
were from religious years;
from the last viceroy, maybe.
It was the work of ancient Jesuits,
a ceiling of oak and camphor,
that exuded a smell of bats
an elderly and withered odor.
Its capricious picture windows
looked out to a manger and corn patch
where the barn swallows used to trill

al balido del recental.
Oíamos arrodillados
los niños desde el coril,
la misa llena de murmurios
y de fresco aroma cerril.
Divisábamos cerro alegre,
por el antiguo tragaluz,
la murmuradora compuerta
y los sauces llenos de luz.
Y llegar oímos un coche
de híspidos galgos al rumor;
dos huéspedes se acercaron
y una niña de Van Dyck flor.
Estaba de blanco vestida,
con verde ceñidor gentil,
su cabello olía a muñeca
y a nítido beso de abril.
Diamante era en luces añosas,
luz en cofre medioeval;
acallaba aroma de cirio,
con su perfume matinal.
Y nos miraba dulcemente
con primaveril sensación,
junto al melodio desflautado
que era de insectos panteón.
Relinchaban en el pesebre
el picazo y el alazán;

to the bleating of the suckling calf.
We were listening on our knees
the children from the choral,
the Mass full of murmuration
and of a fresh untamed aroma.
We sighted happy hill,
through the ancient skylight,
the murmuring floodgate
and the willows full of light.
And arriving we heard a coach
of hollowed greyhounds in whisper;
two of the guests came close
and a girl of Van Dyck flower.
In white she was dressed,
with a green girdle gentle,
her hair smelled like a doll
and like a clear kiss of April.
A diamond was in age-old lights,
light in a medieval chest;
quelling a candle aroma,
with her matinal fragrance.
And with a spring-like sensation
she was staring at us sweetly,
next to the defluted panpipes
that were a graveyard of insects.
Neighing in the manger
the flaxen and the chestnut;

soñamos pasear con ella
a la luz del día galán.
Llevarla ofrecimos, fugaces,
por la toma, por el jardín,
por la cerrada vieja colca
y por de la hacienda el confín.
Sus mejillas se coloreaban
con primaveral multiflor,
sus lindos ojos se dormían
al áureo y tibio resplandor.
Y nos hablaba con dulzura
y cariñosa inquietud;
cundían sueños plateados
al ígneo sol de juventud.
Sonó la campanilla clara
seguida de dulce rumor
de los tábanos. Nuestros padres,
los de ella oraban con fervor.
Al lado, con grandes espuelas,
rezaba ronco el caporal,
y también los peones que saben
misterios del cañaveral.
La acequia de cal y canto
que iba del estanque al jardín,
nos llamaba con el ensueño
de madreselva y de jazmín.
Correr ansiamos con la niña

we dreamed of strolling with her
to the light of the gallant day.
To take her we offered, swiftly,
by the intake, by the garden,
by the old enclosed outhouse
and by the hacienda's confines.
With springtime multiflora
her cheeks were reddening,
in golden and warm resplendency
her pretty eyes were slumbering.
And she spoke to us with sweetness
and affectionate inquisitiveness;
silvery dreams escalated
to the igneous sun of youthfulness.
The handbell rung clearly
followed by the sweet murmur
of the horseflies. Our parents,
hers were praying with fervor.
On the side, with great riding spurs
hoarsely the herdsman was praying,
and also the peons who know
about the mysteries of the reedbed.
The gutter of limewash and pebbles
that went from fountain to garden,
was calling us with the daydream
of honeysuckle and jasmine.
To run with the girl we were eager

y en camelote navegar,
para sentir, al aire verde,
un repentino naufragar.
Y salvarnos en la isla rosa,
vivienda del insecto azul,
como en el árbol de los cuentos
donde canta el dulce bulbul.
O llegar a gruta vistosa
con los brillos del zacuaral,
que habita el hada del estanque,
que es una garza virreinal.
Mas ella lanzó agudo grito
a un pajizo reptil zancón,
y los orantes la rodearon
blancos de desesperación.
En su cara sombras de muerte
y de amargura descubrí:
tenía en la pierna celeste
un negro y triste rubí.

and to sail on a water hyacinth,
to feel, all of a sudden,
a shipwrecking, on the green wind.
And be saved in the rosy island,
housing of the insect blue,
as on the fairytale tree
wherein sings the sweet bulbul.
Or to reach an alluring grotto
with the pampas grass' glimmers,
inhabited by the pond fairy,
which is a viceroyal heron.
Yet she cried out a sharp scream
at a reptile straw-colored and lanky
and the prayerful surrounded her
by desperation whitened.
On her face shadows of death
and of bitterness I discovered:
she had on her celestial leg
a black and sorrowful ruby.

LIED V

La canción del adormido cielo
dejó dulces pesares;
yo quisiera dar vida a esa canción
que tiene tanto de ti.
Ha caído la tarde sobre el musgo
del cerco inglés,
con aire de otro tiempo musical.
El murmurio de la última fiesta
ha dejado colores tristes y suaves
cual de primaveras obscuras
y listones perlinos.
Y las dolidas notas
han traído melancolía
de las sombras galantes
al dar sus adioses sobre la playa.
La celestía de tus ojos dulces
tiene un pesar de canto,
que el alma nunca olvidará.
El ángel de los sueños te ha besado
para dejarte amor sentido y musical
y cuyos sones de tristeza
llegan al alma mía,
como celestes miradas

LIED V

The song of the slumbering heavens
left behind sweet regrets;
I would like to give life to that song
which has so much of you.
The afternoon has fallen over the moss
of the English fence,
with airs of another musical time.
The murmuring of the last festivity
has left behind sad and soft colors
like those of obscure springtimes
and pearly ribbons.
And the afflicted notes
have brought in the melancholy
of the gallant shadows
while giving their goodbyes over the beach.
The celesty of your sweet eyes
has a songful regret,
that the soul will never forget.
The angel of dreams has given you a kiss
to leave you with heartfelt and musical love
and whose lullabies of sadness
reach to this soul of mine,
like celestial gazes

en esta niebla de profunda soledad.
¡Es la canción simbólica
como un jazmín de sueño,
que tuviera tus ojos y tu corazón!
¡Yo quisiera dar vida a esta canción!

on this fog of profound solitude.
It is the symbolic song
like a dreamy jasmine,
that would have your eyes and your heart!
I would like to give life to this song!

PEREGRÍN CAZADOR DE FIGURAS

En el mirador de la fantasía,
al brillar del perfume
tembloroso de harmonía;
en la noche que llamas consume;
cuando duerme el ánade implume,
los órficos insectos se abruman
y luciérnagas fuman;
cuando lucen los silfos galones, entorcho
y vuelan mariposas de corcho
o los rubios vampiros cecean,
o las firmes jorobas campean;
por la noche de los matices,
de ojos muertos y largas narices;
en el mirador distante,
por las llanuras;
Peregrín cazador de figuras,
con ojos de diamante
mira desde las ciegas alturas.

PEREGRIN HUNTER OF FIGURES

On the overlook of fantasy,
under the glow of perfume
trembling with harmony;
in the night that by flames is consumed;
when the featherless mallard sleeps,
the orphic insects are overwhelmed
and the fireflies puff and swell;
when the sylphs are flaunting insignias, braids
and cork butterflies are flying away
or the blond vampires are stuttering,
or the firm humps are wandering;
through the night of nuances,
of dead eyes and long noses;
on the distant overlook,
through the pastures;
Peregrin hunter of figures,
with eyes of diamond
gazes from the blind altitudes.

MEDIOEVAL

En un sueño vienen claras sensaciones florentinas:
el bullicio se acentúa de la ronda callejera,
y repiten sus estrofas en las dulces mandolinas
los mancebos y los pajes que transitan por la acera.

Ya de alegres nubecillas se engalana el firmamento,
ya despuntan de belleza los matices mundanales;
y ora tienen los bastiones colorado paramento
y se asoman las doncellas y floridos barandales.

Palaciegos adornados con plumajes y caireles,
se confunden en los coros donde lloran los maitines;
y resuenan en sus flancos las hebillas y broqueles,
y, en el duro pavimento, los tendidos espolines.

En la plaza se perfilan los gentiles caballeros,
van llegando embajadores que de brillos alardean,
y tras ellos arrogantes paladines extranjeros
en sus yeguas tunecinas que briosas escarcean.

Por la vía que perfuman mirabeles deliciosos,
ves galanes y doncellas en sus rápidas monturas,
los semblantes, los cabellos tienen brillos misteriosos,
tienen brillos misteriosos pavonadas armaduras.

MEDIEVAL

On a dream are coming Florentine sensations clearly:
the ballyhoo of the rambling round accentuates,
and repeating their stanzas on the mandolins sweetly
young fellows and attendants traversing the walkway.

Now with happy little clouds the firmament is embellished,
now with beauty are burgeoning the worldly shadings;
and heretofore the bastions have the trappings reddish
and peeking out are the maidens and the flowery handrails.

Palace dwellers adorned with crystal beads and feathers,
are confused in the choirs where they groan the morning prayers;
and resounding in their flanks the buckles and the bucklers,
and, in the hard pavement, the riding spurs splayed.

In the plaza are shaping up the gentlemen genteel,
ambassadors that boast about their sparkles are arriving,
and behind them arrogant foreigner paladins
on their Tunisian mares that spirited are prancing.

By the road that is perfumed by delicious mirabelles,
you see dandies and maidens on their speedy saddles,
the countenances, the hairs have mysterious sparkles,
mysterious sparkles have the passivated armors.

Junto al Arno, dulce ahora florecido y halagüeño,
las beldades nos parecen de la Loggia las teorías;
y son notas de perfume, son las hijas del ensueño,
son la mística dulzura de las muertas alegrías.

Y esas reinas ideales con su velo matutino,
ya se postran, ya contemplan la madona del retablo;
y los jóvenes campeones y el anciano gibelino
fuscos llevan en la cota, junto al pecho, su venablo.

Y ellos saben los silencios de los seres adorables,
en los húmedos rincones donde gime el ermitaño,
y conocen los enigmas de las almas incurables,
los enigmas de la noche, de la muerte y del engaño.

Y esos Grandes circundados de los bélicos colores,
también sufren del Ocaso tristes nubes amarillas;
ve los condes retorcidos en deliquios tembladores,
ve las damas y los reyes; todo el mundo de rodillas.

Y la tarde ya desciende, y en el claustro denegrido,
los ascetas dan al cielo su agonía ¡dura suerte!,
y por calles ignoradas va con fúnebre alarido,
va con fúnebre alarido la carroza de la Muerte.

Next to the Arno, sweet now flowered and flattering,
the beauties seem to us like the theories of the Lodge;
and they are perfume notes, they are the daughters of daydream,
they are the mystic sweetness of the deceased joys.

And those ideal queens with their matutinal veil,
now prostrate, now contemplate the Madonna of the altar;
and the champion young ones and the Ghibelline old man
bedimmed carry on the chain mail, next to the chest, their darts.

And they know the silence of the adorable beings,
in the humid corners wherein moans the hermit,
and they cognize the enigmas of incurable souls,
the enigmas of the night, of death and of deceit.

And those Great ones encircled by the bellicose colors,
also suffer from the Sundown's sorrowful yellow clouds;
behold the twisted counts in their trembling raptures,
behold the ladies and the kings; everyone kneeling down.

And the evening now descends, and in the blackened monk's cell,
the ascetics give their agony to heaven, tough fate!,
and it goes by ignored streets with a funereal yell,
it goes with a funereal yell the carriage of Death.

AVATARA

Resonaban los dulces orfeones...
pintó el farolero,
violeta lucero,
y vimos tristeza clara en los balcones.

En la mística muerte del día
se brumó la Luna, con tinte sagrado,
y sentí de la almea sombría
esos ojos que nunca han amado.

En el hondo cantar zahareño,
del canal perlino en la nube salobre,
me decía lugares de ensueño,
con las rubias monedas de cobre.

Al brillar de la luz veneciana,
fatal de la feria galante ha reído;
es la blonda, es la negra indostana
de los ojos que siempre han dormido.

Hoy es implacable la desconocida...
el azul hirviente nubló las mamparas,
la feria encendida...
¡Ay, las avataras!
¡Ay, aquellos ojos nocturnos, sin vida!

AVATAR

The sweet chorales were resounding...
the lamplighter painted,
a bright star in violet,
and we saw a clear sadness on the balconies.

On the mystical death of the day
with a sacred tinge, the Moon has gloomed,
and of the somber Almeh I felt
those eyes that never have loved.

In the deep obstreperous singing,
of the pearly canal in the salty cloud,
would tell me of places in dreaming,
with the blond minted copper crowns.

Under the glow of the Venetian light,
it's the blonde one, it's the black Hindustani;
fatally about the gallant fair has laughed
with the eyes that have always been asleep.

The unknown one is relentless today...
the boiling blue has clouded the shutters,
ignited is the fair...
Oh, the avatars!
Oh, those nocturnal eyes, without life!

MARCHA ESTIVA

Hay de rosáceas un puente
en los cerros luminados,
siempre lejano.

Y en el alba de placeres,
las vírgenes lo pasaban
dulces y claras.

Por las alturas las fuentes
decían, en versos magos,
azul retrato.

Sobre abismos, sobre edenes,
las núbiles pintorescas
soñaban ciegas.

¿Adónde van las celestes
cuando, en las estivas nubes,
duermen las luces?

ESTIVAL MARCH

There is of rosebuds a bridge
in the luminated hills,
always far away.

And in the dawn of pleasures,
the virgins were biding time
sweetly and clearly.

On the highlands the fountains
were telling, in magic verses,
of a blue portrait.

Of abysses, of edens
the picturesque nubile ones
were dreaming blindly.

Where do the celestials go
when, on the estival clouds
are sleeping the lights?

EFÍMERA

Da vespertino rayo la zarca luna,
ronda efímera verde por la laguna.

Por las aguas doradas dichosa vuelas
celebrando la vida, con tarantelas.

Ya miras las luciolas de los jardines,
y en ribereñas casas los lamparines.

Y en tu vuelo, soñando buscas la orquesta
de la luz nacarina por la floresta.

Ni temes las cercanas plomizas lluvias;
y en la laguna gozas las fiestas rubias.

Y desoyes la culpa de las ninfeas
por los juegos de amores que centelleas.

En tus celos las alas tiendes veloces
a la naciente imagen que desconoces.

Tú, ideal tempranero que el mundo invoca,
dejas tanta hermosura por fuga loca.

Y sueñas instintiva o iluminada
en la luz de la muerte. ¡Flor de la nada!

EPHEMERAL

The pale blue moon gives a vespertine ray,
ephemeral green round dance by the lake.

By the golden waters cheerful you fly
with tarantellas, celebrating life.

Now in the gardens you watch the fireflies,
and in riverside houses the lamplights.

And in your flight, for the orchestra you aim
in a dream of the pearly light by the glade.

You do not fear the nearby grayish rains;
in the lake you enjoy the blond holidays.

And you dismiss the fault of the nymphets
due to the games of love you scintillate.

In your jealousy you spread your wings fast
to the rising image you don't recognize.

You, early ideal invoked by the world,
leave so much beauty the mad flight along.

And you dream instinctive or illuminated,
flower of nothing!, in the light of death.

NOCHE I

Es la noche de amargura;
¡qué callada, qué dormida!
la ciudad de la locura;
la ciudad de los fanales
clamorosos, de las vías funerales,
la mansión de las señales.
En mi estancia denegrida,
mustia, ronca, pavorida,
donde duermen los estantes;
ciegos libros ignorantes,
de la muerte con la esencia están los vasos;
y ora vienen, ora riman,
ora lentos se aproximan
unos pasos, unos pasos.
¡Triste noche!; baja bruma
de arrecida sensación el alma llena;
es la hora que me abruma
con el vivo despertar de mi honda pena;
son las doce, la inserena.
Luna llora; viene aquí la muerte mía,
a la estancia de los tristes cielos rasos;
¡cómo llegan con letal melancolía!,
¡ay, sus pasos!, ¡ay, sus pasos!

NIGHT I

It's the night of bitterness;
so quiet, so asleep!
the city of madness;
the city of the beacons
resounding, of the funeral roads,
the mansion of the signals.
In my blackened bedroom,
withered, hoarse, frightened,
where the bookshelves are sleeping;
books blind and unknowing,
the cups filled with the essence of death;
and now they come, now they rhyme,
now slowly coming near by
someone's steps, someone's steps.
Sorrowful evening!; low brume
with chilled sensation the soul filling;
it's the hour that burdens me
with my deep sorrow's live awakening;
it's twelve o'clock, the restless.
The moon weeps; here comes the death of me,
to the room of the sad open skies;
how they arrive with lethal melancholy!,
Oh, its steps!, Oh, its steps!

Fue de luz tu madrugada,
fue dichosa; recorriste,
por la senda coloreada,
todo un sueño en esta vida que es tan triste,
todo un sueño en esta vida inconsolada.
Infantil y reidora,
noche nunca presintiera,
en el sueño tu alma aurora;
¡fue tu senda encantadora!,
¡tu balada tempranera!;
y hoy en noche aridecida siento pasos
¡ay, tus pasos!, ¡ay, tus pasos!
Y después la puna helada
te vio enferma, nacarada;
y tus risas matinales
se volvieron tristes notas musicales;
y de Schumann vibraciones,
de Chopin tribulaciones
diste al piano, con azules lloros lasos,
como suenan las canciones
de tus pasos, de tus pasos.
Y en tu pálida agonía,
me dijiste que vendría
tu alma a ver la mi esperanza que fenece
en la muda librería
donde Sirio se obscurece;
tu alma a ver mi desventura,

Of light was your early dawning,
it was blissful; you traversed,
through the colorful pathway,
all a dream in this life so full of sadness,
all a dream in this life so brokenhearted.
Childlike and whimsical,
the night would never foretell,
in the dream your soul in dawn;
was your enchanting pathway!,
your early morning ballad!;
and now in a dried-up night I feel steps
Oh, your steps! Oh, your steps!
And then the frozen highlands
saw you sickly, nacre-like;
and your morning time laughs
became sorrowful musical notes;
and Schumann's vibrations,
Chopin's tribulations
you played on the piano, with weary blue tears,
Iike the sound made by the songs
of your steps, of your steps.
And in your pale agony,
there you told me it will be
your soul to see my hope expiring
in the speechless library
where Sirius becomes darkened;
your soul to see my misfortunes,

mi ventana, la ciudad de la locura;
y en la noche quemadora de la mente,
sólo llegan, tristemente,
¡ay, tus pasos!, ¡ay, tus pasos!

my window, the city of madness;
and in the burning night of the mind,
sadly, only they arrive,
Oh, your steps!, Oh, your steps!

LAS NIÑAS DE LUZ

Las niñas de luz
que al sol rodean,
centellean
y sonríen;
como cambiante pedrería,
van por la nube harmonía.
Las niñas del sol,
de albinos cabellos
y purpúrea tez
nadan en ígneos destellos.
Desde un arrebol
su vuelo aseguran,
aterrizar procuran;
y, cual coloridas notas,
mueren en las nublas remotas.
Las niñas de luz
que al sol rodean,
centellean
y sonríen.

THE GIRLS OF LIGHT

The girls of light
whom the sun surround,
scintillate
and smile;
like some shifting jewelry,
they go by the cloud harmony.
The girls of the sun,
with albino hair
and purpureal face
swim in igneous flares.
From an afterglow
they assert their flight,
they make sure to land;
and, like colorful notes,
they die on the blur remote.
The girls of light
whom the sun surround,
scintillate
and smile.

José Maria Eguren
Girl and butterfly
Watercolor: 184 x 124 mm.

«It is impossible to fix a compendial physiognomy of Latin American poetry ».
An interview with José María Eguren.

By César Vallejo

From Lima

The great symbolist of "The God of the Sparkle", says to me with a certain bitterness:

— Oh, how much you have to struggle; how much I have been confronted! When I started, friends with some authority on these things, they always discouraged me. And I, as you understand, was finally beggining to believe that I was wrong. Only, some time later, González Prada celebrated my verse.

As his agile, cordial and deep sinuous voice unties, his eyes, of a hallucinated shadow, seem to search for the memories, and they wander the room slowly.

The poet Eguren is of medium height. On his face, of a noble somewhat toasted white tone, his thirty-six years already babble a few autumn lines. His spontaneous ways, cut out in distinction and fluidity, inspire devotion and sympathy from the first moment.

He speaks to us; and his explanations of some of his symbols suggest to us the rarest of illusions. It occurs to me he is an oriental prince who travels in pursuit of impossible sacred Bayadères.

— Since your first tryouts —I ask him— have your ways been the same as now?

—Yes —he answers me, with lively joy. With a single brief parenthesis of romanticism. Many of Rubén Darío's masteries —he adds— I had them, before they were known here. Only that, until very recently, no newspaper wanted to publish my verses. I, of course, never exposed myself to rejection. But, you know, nobody accepted them.

Later, he relates to me about his long years of literary isolation, which would become so fruitful for Latin American letters.

— And Symbolism has already prevailed in the Americas —he tells me with emphasis and rotundity—. The Symbolism of the phrase, that is, the French one, exists already consolidated in the continent; and as for the Symbolism of thought, it does too, but with very different nuances. For example, my tendency is different from any other, according to González Prada. So, as you see, it is impossible to fix a compendial physiognomy of present Latin American poetry.

Eguren grows excited and is visibly enjoying his talks about art.

He presents me with an aromatic "British" cigar, and between smoke and smoke pass through our lips the names of Goncourt, Flaubert, Leconte de Lisle and some Latin American and national writers, interspersed with some divine and eternal verse.

—You and I have to struggle a lot —he says to me, with a gesture of soft resignation.

—But you have already succeeded in all of the Americas —I argue—. What news do you have from outside?

— In Argentina, Chile, Ecuador, Colombia, I know that they know me and that they reproduce my verses with enthusiams. I also maintain numerous relationships with the intellectuals of those countries. As for the rest, we will see, we will see, because still ...

(Through my mind pass the pain and the genius, misunderstood by their century, of Verlaine, of Poe, of Baudelaire).

— And in Trujillo? —Eguren asks me with lively interest.

I am troubled facing this question; and not finding a way to muddle through it, I toss and turn and change my attitude on the divan, until, at last, as suddenly encouraged by a memory, I reply to him:

— In Trujillo...

Eguren interrupts me, and talks to me about the writers there, friends of mine, for whom he dedicates phrases of enthusiastic praise.

— Besides —he rounds off his words with fine gallantry— Trujillo is an agreeable city for me, and I think it has a lot of culture. I give you my thanks.

When I said goodbye, the day had flown by.

On the way back, I look at Barranco, with its straight streets populated with poplar groves; with its arborescent ferns and pine trees. The chalets, of the most varied styles, display gardens of neat elegance and the lobbies open to the vespertine breezes; the luxurious residences of bourgeois comfort.

The Virgilian hour, turquoise and energetic green. And the sea of rich silver.

César Vallejo
La Semana, Trujillo, No. 2 March 30, 1918

José Maria Eguren
Afternoon prayer
Watercolor: 187 x 125.6 mm.

INDEX OF POEMS

LA NIÑA DE LA LAMPARA AZUL 22
THE GIRL OF THE LAMPLIGHT BLUE 23

LOS ÁNGELES TRANQUILOS 24
THE TRANQUIL ANGELS 25

LA SANGRE 26
THE BLOOD 27

LAS CANDELAS 28
THE CANDLES 29

EL CABALLO 30
THE HORSE 31

NOCTURNO 32
NOCTURNAL 33

LA MUERTE DEL ÁRBOL 36
THE DEATH OF THE TREE 37

MARGINAL 38
MARGINAL 39

EL DIOS CANSADO 42
THE TIRED DEITY 43

LA ORACIÓN DEL MONTE 44
THE PRAYER OF THE HILL 45

ELEGÍA DEL MAR 48
ELEGY OF THE SEA 49

ALMA TRISTEZA 50
SOUL SADNESS 51

FLOR DE AMOR 52
FLOWER OF LOVE 53

LAS NAVES DE LA NOCHE 54
THE VESSELS OF THE NIGHT 55

JEZABEL 56
JEZABEL 57

LOS DELFINES 62
THE DOLPHINS 63

LA NAVE ENFERMA 66
THE DISEASED SHIP 67

NUBES DE ANTAÑO 68
CLOUDS OF YESTERYEAR 69

LAS PUERTAS 70
THE DOORS 71

ANTIGUA 72
ANCIENT 73

LIED V 80
LIED V 81

PEREGRÍN CAZADOR DE FIGURAS 84
PEREGRIN HUNTER OF FIGURES 85

MEDIOEVAL 86
MEDIEVAL 87

AVATARA 90
AVATAR 91

MARCHA ESTIVA 92
ESTIVAL MARCH 93

EFÍMERA 94
EPHEMERAL 95

NOCHE I 96
NIGHT I 97

LAS NIÑAS DE LUZ 102
THE GIRLS OF LIGHT 103

José María Eguren (Lima, 1874 – 1942) remains as one of the most important Peruvian poets of all times. His highly original work marks one of the most interesting transitions between Modernismo and the Avant-garde movements in Latin American poetry. He exerted a major influence on a whole generation of poets, writers and thinkers including José Carlos Mariategui, Cesar Vallejo and Martín Adán. He was also admired and recognized in life as an important poet by figures such as Gabriela Mistral, Juan Ramón Jiménez and Jorge Luis Borges. His complete works are regarded as classics of Latin American literature and have been published in Peru, Argentina, Venezuela and Spain.

José Garay Boszeta (Lima, 1985) is a writer, translator and language laborer, born and raised in Lima, Perú. He studied programs in Economics and Philosophy at the National University of San Marcos in Lima. His work in translation aims to reevaluate Latin American narratives and restore their historical content for English speaking audiences around the world. His current projects include the translation of the works of José María Eguren and Martín Adán, among others. He currently lives in Dallas, Texas with his wife, Erin, and their dogs, Willow and Remy.